D1623830

School Prayer

A History of the Debate

Tricia Andryszewski

—Issues in Focus—

Enslow Publishers, Inc.

44 Fadem Road   PO Box 38
Box 699   Aldershot
Springfield, NJ 07081   Hants GU12 6BP
USA   UK

Library of Congress Cataloging-in-Publication Data

Andryszewski, Tricia, 1956–
    School prayer : a history of the debate / Tricia Andryszewski.
        p.   cm. — (Issues in focus)
    Includes bibliographical references and index.
    ISBN 0-89490-904-5
    1. Prayer in the public schools—Law and legislation—United
States—History. I. Title. II. Series: Issues in focus (Hillside, N.J.)
KF4162.Z9A54 1997
344.73'0796—dc21
                                   96-51951
                                        CIP

Printed in the United States of America

10 9 8 7 6 5 4 3

Illustration Credits: Library of Congress, pp. 6, 11, 14, 18, 20, 26, 31, 39,
42, 44, 47, 50, 53, 61, 67, 76, 80, 86, 90.

Cover Illustration: Enslow Publishers, Inc.

Contents

1

Points of View

Congress shall make no law respecting an establishment of religion, or prohibiting the free exercise thereof; or abridging the freedom of speech, or of the press, or the right of the people peaceably to assemble, and to petition the government for a redress of grievances.

> —First Amendment to the U.S. Constitution, ratified December 15, 1791.

No state law or school board may require that passages from the Bible be read or that the Lord's Prayer be recited in the public schools of a State at the beginning of each school day—even if individual students may be excused from attending or participating in such exercises upon written request of their parents.

> —Justice Tom Clark, writing for the Supreme Court in the 1963 *Abington School District* v. *Schempp* decision.[1]

Alabama Governor George Wallace took a firm stand against Supreme Court decisions that would prevent requiring students to pray and read Bible passages in public schools.

The trend of taking God and moral teaching from the schools is a diabolical scheme.

> —the Reverend Billy Graham, reacting to *Engel* v. *Vitale* and *Schempp.*[2]

I don't care what they say in Washington, we are going to keep right on praying and reading the Bible in the public schools of Alabama.

> —Alabama Governor George Wallace, reacting to *Schempp.*[3]

Our schools aren't there to put values and morals in our kids. That's what [parents] do. If we can't do that, that's what's wrong with the world today, is parents aren't doing their job. It's not up to the school or the school system or a principal or teachers, or anybody else out there. It's up to the parents.

> —Terry Arcola (parent of a high-school student involved in a 1993 school-prayer controversy in Jackson, Mississippi).[4]

The Supreme Court decision in 1963 was a bad law, bad history, and bad culture. . . . And if the Court doesn't want to reverse itself, then we have an absolute obligation to pass a constitutional amendment to instruct the Court on its error.

—Congressman Newt Gingrich, October 1994.[5]

Our Founders understood that religious freedom was basically a coin with two sides. The Constitution protected the free exercise of religion, but prohibited the establishment of religion. It's a careful balance that's uniquely American. It is the genius of the First Amendment. It does not, as some people have implied, make us a religion-free country. It has made us the most religious country in the world.

—President Bill Clinton, July 1995.[6]

2

Church, State, and Public Schools

Separation of church and state—one of the fundamental principles of U.S. government and law—has not always prevailed in America. Before the Revolutionary War, none of the thirteen colonies was fully legally tolerant of all religions. Only in Pennsylvania, for example, was it legal for Roman Catholic priests to say Mass. Dozens of colonial dissenters—from Catholics to Baptists to Quakers—were imprisoned for refusing to fit into the religion expected of them. Some were put to death.

Toward the end of the 1700s, however, general agreement emerged in the British colonies of North America favoring religious tolerance and separation of church and state. There were practical reasons for this change. So many different churches flourished in the colonies that no single dominant religion could be enforced. Furthermore, the colonists' positive experiences in living side by side and doing business (as

8

well as making a revolution) together with fellow
colonists who had diverse points of view made them
more tolerant of religious differences. In addition, for
generations Rhode Island and Pennsylvania had pursued
relatively liberal policies of religious tolerance. The
success of those experiments encouraged other colonies,
and ultimately the Founding Fathers of the new United
States, to move in that direction.

The Age of Reason

There were purely intellectual reasons for the new
consensus as well. The American revolutionaries lived
and dreamed and thought in the intellectual climate of
the Enlightenment, also known as the Age of Reason.
The Western world in the 1700s was a hotbed of science
and learning and inquiry using the then new "scientific
method" (the process of carefully observing and
collecting data about a specific something being studied,
then rigorously testing any conclusions drawn from the
data). The key belief underlying this great expansion of
human knowledge was that the entire universe was an
orderly place governed by "natural laws" (such as the law
of gravity) and that these laws could be discovered by
careful observation and reasoning. The leading thinkers
of the day thus believed that, in an atmosphere of free
thought and debate, the truth—in religion as in
science—would naturally prevail.

Political thinkers in Europe as well as in the North
American colonies sought to apply reason and order and
natural law to the design of government—and to prevent
government from using its authority and power to

9

mandate what its citizens should think and believe. The framers of the U.S. Constitution were particularly influenced by the seventeenth-century English philosopher John Locke, who wrote that:

> *First,* . . . the care of souls is not committed to the civil magistrate, any more than to other men. It is not committed unto him, I say, by God; because it appears not that God has ever given any such authority to one man over another, as to compel any one to his religion. . . .
>
> *In the second place,* The care of souls cannot belong to the civil magistrate because his power consists only in outward force, but true and saving religion consists in the inward persuasion of the mind.[1]

Tolerance and Separation

From the very beginning, the new American consensus about church and state embraced two different but related elements. First was the principle of tolerance: Conflicting religious beliefs should be tolerated by law and by custom. Second was the principle of separation: Government should not be involved with religion.

The distinction between these two is important. Tolerance is achieved when no one is injured by religious intolerance, but separation must be enforced *whether anyone is damaged by a particular government involvement or not.* The framers of the U.S. Constitution believed that to allow government and religion to intermingle would be damaging and corrupting for both, in addition to any specific damage the intermingling might inflict on particular individuals or religious organizations. Because

Thomas Jefferson believed that the United States Constitution and the idea of the separation of church and state forbid the government from meddling in religious matters in any way.

of this, it wasn't enough for government to favor or disfavor all religions evenhandedly. Separation of church and state required that government not meddle in religion at all.

Although the phrase "separation of church and state" appears nowhere in the Constitution, the idea and even the words themselves were nonetheless fixed in the minds of its authors. Thomas Jefferson, for example, while he was president referred to the First Amendment as "building a wall of separation between church and state."[2]

The principles of tolerance and separation were considered so basic and obviously inherent in the main body of the Constitution, even before the Bill of Rights was added, that many of the Founding Fathers saw no need to write them out explicitly in the First Amendment. As Alexander Hamilton put it: "Why declare that things shall not be done which there is no power to do?"[3]

The Establishment and Free Exercise Clauses

Nonetheless, both principles became enshrined in the First Amendment: "Congress shall make no law respecting an establishment of religion [separation], or prohibit the free exercise thereof [religious tolerance]." These two clauses, known as the Establishment Clause and the Free Exercise Clause, have been at the heart of the legal controversies about school prayer.

The First Amendment originally restricted only Congress, the national legislature. For many years state legislatures could (and many did) make laws intervening in religious matters. In 1868, however, the Fourteenth Amendment to the Constitution established that:

> No State shall make or enforce any law which shall abridge the privileges or immunities of citizens of the United States; nor shall any State deprive any person of life, liberty, or property without due process of law; nor deny to any person within its jurisdiction the equal protection of the laws.

Although the Fourteenth Amendment was originally intended (at the end of the Civil War) to put an end to state laws permitting slavery in Southern states, over many years it has come to mean much more than that. It has come to mean that state governments, no less than the federal government, must respect the freedoms and rights specified in the Constitution—including the clauses concerning freedom of religion. In a series of legal cases in the 1920s, 1930s, and 1940s, the Supreme Court firmly established that state governments, too, must obey the First Amendment's required separation of church and state.

Public Education and Religion

Throughout all this time, public education across the United States continued to include considerable religious content, as it had since colonial times. For example, in colonial New England, whose locally controlled public schools became the model for public schools throughout the United States, the earliest standard text was the *New England Primer*, which taught younger children to read and count using biblical references: The letter *A* was

13

By the 1940s, the Supreme Court had established that the states as well as the federal government must respect the rights and freedoms granted by the United States Constitution.

taught with the phrase "In *Adam's* Fall we sinned all," and *P* was illustrated with "*Peter* denies His Lord and cries."

According to the legal scholar Leo Pfeffer, who as chief legal counsel for the American Jewish Congress played a key role in many cases before the Supreme Court dealing with separation of church and state:

> Public education in the United States rests on three fundamental assumptions: First, that the legislature has the power to tax all—even the childless and those whose children attend private schools—in order to provide free public education for all; second, that the legislature has the power to require every parent to provide for his children a basic education in secular subjects; third, that the education provided by the state in the free schools must be secular. None of these assumptions was accepted without a struggle.[4]

The first two of these assumptions were generally accepted across the United States by the mid-1800s. The third assumption—that public school education should be secular (not religious)—remains controversial even today. Should students be taught religion-based values? Whose values? Under what circumstances, and using whose words, may students pray?

The struggle over the issue of secular public schools has been going on for well over two hundred years. The issue of prayer in the schools has often been at the center of the debate.

Over many years, the meaning of "secular," as applied to public schools, has changed. In the beginning, it meant simply that schools were controlled by government officials, rather than by church officials. No

15

single religious organization thus controlled the schools. But since the vast majority of United States citizens were Protestant Christians, Protestant values—and to some extent Protestant religious content—set the agenda for public schools. Bible reading and prayers, both of a distinctly Protestant flavor, were a normal daily activity in most public schools. Roman Catholics, Jews, and other religious minorities, and Christians who used versions of the Bible different from the King James Version favored by many Protestant churches objected. Many felt out of place in their own public schools. Some also felt they were being pressured to practice Protestant religion in conflict with their families' own religious beliefs.

In the mid-1800s, many Roman Catholics were violently persecuted when they objected to the version of the Bible being used (usually the Protestant King James Version) in public schools. Finding the public schools hostile to their faith, many Catholic parents took their children out of the public schools and enrolled them in the growing network of private schools run by their church.

Beginning around 1913 and continuing through the first half of the twentieth century, state governments across the country decided to standardize and write into law the practice of Bible reading and prayer in their states' public schools. By mid-century, nearly all of the states permitted some form of Bible reading or formal prayer (usually the Lord's Prayer) in public schools. Many states actually *required* Bible reading or prayer, typically with two provisions: (1) that the Bible passages or prayer should be read without comment by any teacher, to avoid sectarian proselytizing (preaching the beliefs of one specific religious faith); and (2) that students whose parents objected to the practice should not have to participate.

Organized religious opinion about school prayer and Bible reading divided along the lines between different faiths. Right up through the 1950s, spokespersons for nearly all Protestant churches favored it. Jewish spokespersons nearly universally opposed it. Years later, a lawyer active in freedom-of-religion cases movingly described his experiences growing up Jewish in public schools where formal prayers were recited:

> My parents, and thousands of other Jews, came to this country from Eastern Europe seeking to enjoy the promise of liberty in a land where there was no officially sanctioned religion, where the possibilities for their children would not be limited by their ancestral faith.
>
> That promise was only partially fulfilled when I was growing up. Let there be no mistake, I am more grateful than words permit me to express for the partial religious liberty that even the America of my youth afforded. But partial liberty was not what we should accept. Let me recall to you what the public schools I attended were like. They had an overtly Protestant cast. Prayers and Bible passages were recited daily. Prayer is not a generic form of expression and Bible passages (and translations) were not, are not, and should not be, theologically neutral. The public school religion I encountered had in every case specific theological roots and forms. The prayers said in the public school I attended were distinctly Protestant in content. The students in the schools I

Through most of the first half of the twentieth century, almost all of the states allowed or required some form of Bible reading or prayer in their public schools.

attended were largely Jewish; the prayers exclusively Christian.

This disparity was no coincidence, nor was it simple ignorance, or even a lingering cultural tradition from a prior generation of students, teachers and school administrators. The use of Protestant religion was a part of a deliberate effort by the public schools to suggest to the American children of Jewish immigrants that these Protestant rituals represented true Americanism, that the rituals and rhythms of our parents' houses were alien and foreign, worse, to children who desperately wished to be accepted, even "un-American." This use of religion as a means of acculturating aliens caused many painful gaps between parent and child.

The Jewish experience is hardly unique. A century earlier, Catholic immigrant children faced the same difficulties.[5]

In keeping with that history, official voices of the Roman Catholic Church for many years opposed school prayer and Bible reading. But they began to change their view after two Supreme Court decisions were handed down in 1947 and 1948: *Everson* v. *Board of Education* (dealing with public transportation for students of private religious schools) and *McCollum* v. *Board of Education* (dealing with the practice of allowing public school students time off from school for religious education). In these decisions, the court emphasized that the First Amendment was intended to build a "wall of separation between church and state"—a concept that the Catholic Church at the time disapproved of heartily. Nonetheless, at about the same time as these court

19

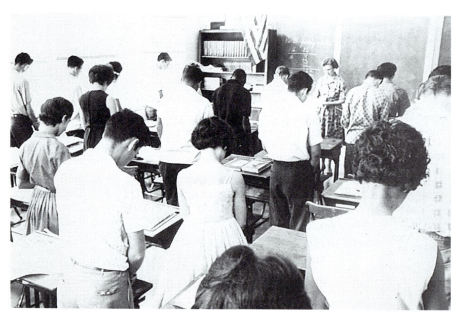

By the early 1960s, religious exercises were taking place in many, perhaps most, public schools across America.

decisions, more and more public schools were demonstrating a willingness to allow Catholic children to use the church-approved Douay Version of the Bible (instead of the King James Version) in schoolroom Bible reading and prayer exercises. By the early 1960s, the Catholic Church had come to strongly favor religious exercises in public schools.

The Lord's Prayer

By that time, religious exercises were regularly conducted in many, perhaps most, public schools across the country. Most often, they took place during that part of the school day set aside for school-related announcements and the Pledge of Allegiance to the U.S. flag. The most common religious exercises were the reading of Bible passages (either by a teacher or by a designated student or students, and either in each classroom or school-wide, over the public address system) and the recital of the Lord's Prayer (usually by all students in unison, with their heads bowed). At some schools, religious hymns were sung. These practices varied greatly from state to state and among different schools within a state.

Most people approved of these practices in their public schools. Some did not. The American Civil Liberties Union, which over the years has been involved in many court challenges to prayer in public schools, explains some of the reasons why some students and parents have been uncomfortable with "officially organized and sponsored devotional exercises in the public school setting":

> Such exercises make children feel they must participate or face the disdain of their teachers and

21

fellow students. Children whose religious beliefs are different from those of the majority must not be made to feel like outsiders in their schools.

Official school prayer also usurps the right of parents to determine if, how, when, where and to whom their children should pray. When schools sponsor prayer or any other religious activity, they infringe on parents' right to choose the religious tradition in which to raise their children. Muslim, Jewish or Hindu parents don't want their children to participate in Christian observances. Atheist parents don't want their children to pray at all. Parents should not have to fear that the public schools are indoctrinating their children in beliefs that run counter to their [families'] beliefs.[6]

By the 1950s, school prayer was commonly practiced throughout the United States—but not entirely accepted. America had always been religiously diverse, and was becoming more so. Furthermore, only about half of the population at the time belonged formally to any church or other religious institution. Some students and their parents were undoubtedly uncomfortable with the practice of school prayer—and a few went to court to challenge it.

3

Engel v. *Vitale* and *Abington* v. *Schempp*

Dozens of legal challenges to school prayer swirled through state and federal courts in the early 1960s. Eventually, one made its way to the Supreme Court, which startled the nation by ruling firmly against the widespread practice of making such a religious exercise part of the regular public-school day.

Engel v. *Vitale*

Engel v. *Vitale*, handed down by the Supreme Court on June 25, 1962, decreed that:

> State officials may not compose an official state prayer and require that it be recited in the public schools of the State at the beginning of each school day—even if the prayer is denominationally neutral [favors no particular religion] and pupils who wish to do so may remain silent or be excused from the room while the prayer is being recited.[1]

On the face of it, *Engel* dealt only with a New York State policy recommending that a simple prayer be said at the beginning of each day in public high schools. Not only did the State Board of Regents (the state agency responsible for public schools) direct that prayer be said, but also they wrote the words to be used: "Almighty God, we acknowledge our dependence upon Thee, and we beg Thy blessings upon us, our parents, our teachers, and our Country."[2]

In its full effect, however, *Engel* challenged long-standing policy and practice in public schools across the country. Nearly two dozen state attorneys general signed on to a friends-of-the-court (*amici curiae*) brief urging the Supreme Court to allow New York's state-mandated school prayer to continue.

The *Engel* case grew out of a decision by a local school board in New York to require that public school students be led in reciting the Regents' prayer each morning after the Pledge of Allegiance to the flag. Parents of several schoolchildren in the district objected and in January 1959 went to court to discontinue the classroom prayers. (By their own description, two of the parents were "of the Jewish faith. One belongs to the Society for Ethical Culture. One is a member of the Unitarian Church. And one is a non-believer."[3]) The following September, the schools issued a new rule allowing any student to be excused from the prayer exercise if his or her parent made such a request in writing. The parents who had started the lawsuit nonetheless decided to continue their efforts to eliminate the prayer exercise entirely, and their case eventually made its way to the Supreme Court.

Arguments Against School Prayer

The lawyers for the parents (the "petitioners" in this case) made a straightforward argument that the recital of the Regents' prayer should not be allowed because the United States Constitution requires separation of church and state. The prayer, they said, violates the Establishment Clause by promoting specific religious beliefs and forms of worship. In addition, the lawyers noted, the prayer conflicts with the religious beliefs of the petitioners. Furthermore, the Regents' prayer "is not part of any national 'tradition' or 'heritage'" unlike, for example, "In God We Trust," which is stamped on U.S. coins. Instead, the lawyers insisted, "it is part of a recognized drive in this country to introduce religious education and observances in public schools." By introducing the Regents' prayer into the public schools, they said, the state clearly intended to aid religion. The state even went so far as to allow state officials themselves to write the words of the prayer—obviously violating the separation of church and state, according to the lawyers. Perhaps worst of all, though, is "the element of coercion" (force) involved. The lawyers noted that not only do students have to attend school but also they have to say the Regents' prayer unless they get special permission not to say it. Even if they do get permission not to say it, they may not leave the classroom. And all students clearly get the message that their school officials, "including their teachers, advocate certain religious beliefs." For all of

In the *Engel* v. *Vitale* decision, Justice Hugo Black spoke for the Supreme Court, ruling that the practice of reciting prayers in public schools was a violation of the Constitution's Establishment Clause.

these reasons, the lawyers concluded, the practice of saying the Regents' prayer "rejects the belief on which the 'Founding Fathers' built our national government, belief in the necessity for absolute separation of church and state. It threatens not merely to breach the 'wall of separation,' but to undermine it completely."[4]

Arguments for School Prayer

Lawyers for the school district and for other state officials disagreed with these arguments. They insisted that no students were being "subjected in the schools to any sectarian or other formal religious teaching." Furthermore, they said that what the parents who brought the case were really trying to do was to completely remove any recognition of God from public schools. "They attack not merely the Regents' prayer but any form of prayer whatsoever," the school's lawyers said.

> They deny to every public school the right to suggest to any child that God is our Creator and the Author of our liberties or to encourage any public expression of gratitude to Him for those liberties, regardless of the wishes of the child or his parents and regardless of the historical and constitutional tradition of this nation.[5]

Continuing, the school officials' lawyers summarized their argument in favor of reciting the Regents' prayer: The Establishment Clause does not forbid public prayer, nor does the Regents' prayer violate the separation of church and state. Public prayer, "part of our national heritage," has been a longstanding tradition in New York and elsewhere in the United States. For these reasons,

Voluntary expressions of belief in God should not be abolished because they are allegedly in conflict with the beliefs of some; . . . those who object because of an alleged conflict with their belief should be permitted to refrain from participating, . . . but there should not be an abolition of such voluntary recital.[6]

The *Engel* Decision

The Supreme Court rejected the New York officials' reasoning and sided with Engel and the other petitioners. Its decision became the law of the land, effectively outlawing this kind of formal prayer exercise in all U.S. public schools. Writing for the Court's majority, Justice Hugo Black was emphatic: "We think that by using its public school system to encourage recitation of the Regents' prayer, the State of New York has adopted a practice wholly inconsistent with the Establishment Clause."[7]

Justice Black continued:

There can, of course, be no doubt that New York's program of daily classroom invocation of God's blessings as prescribed in the Regents' prayer is a religious activity. . . . We think that the constitutional prohibition against laws respecting an establishment of religion must at least mean that in this country it is no part of the business of government to compose official prayers for any group of the American people to recite as a part of a religious program carried on by government.[8]

Black emphasized that the Regents' prayer exercise violated the Constitution no matter whether it favored one religion over another or not. It didn't even matter, Black wrote, whether students were coerced by the prayer exercise or not. The reasons these factors didn't matter have to do with why the Establishment Clause was written into law in the first place. Its chief purpose, according to Black,

> rested on the belief that a union of government and religion tends to destroy government and to degrade religion. . . . [It] thus stands as an expression of principle on the part of the Founders of our Constitution that religion is too personal, too sacred, too holy, to permit its "unhallowed perversion" [in the words of James Madison] by a civil magistrate.[9]

Black also noted that the Establishment Clause was written by lawmakers who were very much aware

> of the historical fact that governmentally established religions and religious persecutions go hand in hand. . . . It was in large part to get completely away from this sort of systematic religious persecution that the Founders brought into being our Nation, our Constitution, and our Bill of Rights with its prohibition against any governmental establishment of religion. The New York laws officially prescribing the Regents' prayer are inconsistent both with the purposes of the Establishment Clause and with the Establishment Clause itself.[10]

Black specifically rejected the school officials' claim that the petitioners were attacking not only the Regents'

29

prayer but all prayer. Their argument against the Regents' prayer did not, Black wrote,

> indicate a hostility toward religion or toward prayer. Nothing, of course, could be more wrong. . . . It is neither sacrilegious nor antireligious to say that each separate government in this country should stay out of the business of writing or sanctioning official prayers and leave that purely religious function to the people themselves and to those the people choose to look to for religious guidance.[11]

The *Schempp* Cases

Almost exactly one year later, on June 17, 1963, the Supreme Court, in *School District of Abington Township, Pennsylvania, et al.* v. *Schempp et al.* ruled that:

> No state law or school board may require that passages from the Bible be read or that the Lord's Prayer be recited in the public schools of a State at the beginning of each school day—even if individual students may be excused from attending or participating in such exercises upon written request of their parents.[12]

The Schempp case was actually two cases: *School District of Abington Township, Pennsylvania, et al.* v. *Schempp et al.* and *Murray et al.* v. *Curlett et al.* These two cases were similar enough that the Supreme Court decided to rule on them together in one opinion.

In the first of these cases, Edward Schempp and his wife, Sidney Schempp, had objected to their children's

Edward Schempp (wearing hat, at left) challenged the practice of reading Bible verses over the public address system in his children's public school.

public school's daily practice of reading Bible verses over a public address system, followed by the recital of the Lord's Prayer by all students not excused from participating at their parents' request. Usually the King James Version of the Bible was used, although sometimes the student giving the reading chose to use the Douay Version or the Torah (Jewish scripture) instead. The Schempps, Unitarians, found that some of the material read to the children conflicted with the family's religious beliefs.

In response to the Schempps' challenge, the state changed its law to read: "At least ten verses from the Holy Bible shall be read, without comment, at the opening of each public school on each school day. Any child shall be excused from such Bible reading, or attending such Bible reading, upon the written request of his parent or guardian."[13] The Schempps believed that having their children excused might harm their relationships with teachers and classmates, a choice they did not find acceptable. They continued to pursue their efforts to end the Bible reading. Eventually, their case made its way to the Supreme Court, where it joined the *Murray* case.

The *Murray* Case

At issue in *Murray* was the city of Baltimore's treatment of a Maryland law concerning "opening exercises" in public schools. The law specified that "each school, either collectively or in classes, shall be opened by the reading, without comment, of a chapter in the Holy Bible and/or the use of the Lord's Prayer."[14]

A student in a Baltimore school, William J. Murray,

III, and his mother, Madalyn Murray, both professed atheists, unsuccessfully tried to have the school board put an end to this religious exercise. In response to their efforts, the rules for opening exercises were changed to read: "Any child shall be excused from participating in the opening exercises or from attending the opening exercises upon the written request of his parent or guardian." The Murrays rejected the changed rule as well and pressed to have the religious exercise stopped altogether, claiming that:

> It threatens their religious liberty by placing a premium on belief as against non-belief and subjects their freedom of conscience to the rule of the majority; it pronounces belief in God as the source of all moral and spiritual values, equating these values with religious values, and thereby renders sinister, alien and suspect the beliefs and ideals of [the Murrays], promoting doubt and question of their morality, good citizenship and good faith.[15]

The Supreme Court's Decision

The Schempps' lawyers argued that the public school Bible reading violated both the Establishment Clause and the Free Exercise Clause of the First Amendment—and that it did so even though students could be excused from the Bible reading. The lawyers said that the Schempp family's

> constitutionally guaranteed rights to the free exercise of religion includes complete freedom to shape and mold the religious orientation of their minor

children. . . . Much that is promulgated by the King James Version is contrary to the religious beliefs and teaching of the [Schempps] and some is personally offensive to them. In order to be free of interference by the state in the religious training of their children [the Schempps] are required, by the written excuse provision, to profess publicly a belief or disbelief and to label publicly and identify their children on each day of the school year as dissenters.[16]

The school officials responsible for the Bible-reading exercises in these cases disagreed. In their brief to the Supreme Court, the Pennsylvania officials' lawyers contended that no students were forced to participate and that the Bible reading did not prevent any students or their parents from freely exercising their religious beliefs. The Bible reading wasn't even a "religious practice," the school officials' lawyers said.

It requires only that those who wish to do so may listen to daily readings without discussion or comment from a great work that possesses many values, including religious, moral, literary and historical. . . . [It] does not involve proselytizing, persuasion, or religious indoctrination. It involves no avowal of faith, acceptance of doctrine, or statement of belief. Listening to the Bible being read . . . is not a religious act.

Even if there were religious content to the Bible reading, the school officials' lawyers argued, that would not necessarily mean that the practice must be outlawed. The Supreme Court itself, the lawyers noted,

has affirmed that we are a religious people. . . .
Nothing in the Constitution requires that the courts
or the government should be hostile to religion. . . .
This Court is not required, under the First
Amendment, to eradicate from this nation's public
life all voluntary customs and established traditions
which some might consider to have religious
connotations.

Not only would outlawing public-school Bible
reading be hostile to religion, according to the school
officials' lawyers, but also it would blaze a trail, they
warned, for future hostility to the traditional role of
religion in public life:

A decision by this Court that the Pennsylvania Bible
reading practice is unconstitutional would provide a
precedent whereby there could be eliminated from
the public life of this nation all those customs and
traditions that evidence the religious nature and
origin of our country and are now and have long been
cherished and accepted by a vast majority of the
people.[17]

The Supreme Court disagreed with the arguments of
the school and state officials and ruled that the Bible-
reading exercises in question were unconstitutional.
Writing for the Court's majority, Justice Tom Clark
emphasized that both the Establishment Clause and the
Free Exercise Clause of the First Amendment require
government "neutrality" concerning religion. In order for
a law to meet the standards of the Establishment Clause,
Justice Clark wrote, it must have a nonreligious purpose

and "a primary effect that neither advances nor inhibits religion." Looking at the school exercises at issue in *Schempp* and *Murray,* Justice Clark decided that they were in fact religious ceremonies created by state officials for the clearly religious purpose of advancing religion. On both counts then, Clark wrote, "the exercises and the law requiring them are in violation of the Establishment Clause."[18]

Justice Clark specifically rejected several arguments in defense of the religious exercises. "It is no defense," he wrote, "to urge that the religious practices here may be relatively minor encroachments on the First Amendment. The breach of neutrality that is today a trickling stream may all too soon become a raging torrent and, in the words of [James] Madison, 'it is proper to take alarm at the first experiment on our liberties.'" (Madison and other founders of the United States didn't want to give up even a little bit of the freedom they had fought so hard to enshrine in the Constitution.) Justice Clark also rejected the claim that "unless these religious exercises are permitted a 'religion of secularism' is established in the schools."[19]

Furthermore, Clark noted: "It certainly may be said that the Bible is worthy of study for its literary and historic qualities." He emphasized that the First Amendment does not forbid students from studying religions or the Bible as part of a secular public school education. Finally, Clark concluded that:

> The place of religion in our society is an exalted one, achieved through a long tradition of reliance on the home, the church and the inviolable citadel of the

36

individual heart and mind. We have come to recognize through bitter experience that it is not within the power of government to invade that citadel, whether its purpose or effect be to aid or oppose, to advance or retard. In the relationship between man and religion, the State is firmly committed to a position of neutrality.[20]

4

Reaction

In the decades after World War II, the United States became caught up in a great movement to promote liberty, equality, and justice for all of its citizens. Beginning with the gains made by the African-American civil rights movement in the 1950s and 1960s, minorities—blacks, women, Latinos, homosexuals, and others—fought for and won access to many opportunities and freedom from much harmful discrimination.

The U.S. Supreme Court during the years it was led by Chief Justice Earl Warren (1953–1969) gave many of these gains the force of law. The Warren Court's long series of landmark decisions included *Brown* v. *Board of Education of Topeka* (1954), which outlawed racial segregation in public schools. The Court's decisions protecting religious minorities in the 1962 and 1963

Earl Warren served as Chief Justice of the Supreme Court from 1953
to 1969, turbulent years for the issue of prayer in schools.

school-prayer cases can be seen as part of this wider, history-making trend.

Congress's Reaction to *Engel*

These landmark changes did not proceed without opposition—including opposition from many of the nation's top politicians. Congress's reaction to the Supreme Court's decision in *Engel* v. *Vitale* (1962) was immediate and overwhelmingly negative. Members of Congress proposed various amendments to the U.S. Constitution intended to counter the *Engel* decision, including one introduced by Representative Frank Becker (R-N.Y.) the day after the decision was handed down: "Prayers shall be offered in the course of any program in any public school or other public place in the United States."[1]

Many members of Congress talked about the *Engel* decision as if it were an attack against God himself. According to Senator Herman Talmadge of Georgia, *Engel* was "an outrageous edict which has numbed the conscience and shocked the highest sensibilities of the nation." Representative John Bell Williams of Mississippi called it "a deliberate and carefully planned conspiracy to substitute materialism for spiritual values."[2]

The President

In contrast to the negative reaction in Congress, President John F. Kennedy offered a calmer point of view. As the first Roman Catholic ever to be elected president of the United States, Kennedy was particularly sensitive to issues concerning separation of church and state. At a press conference, he said:

> The Supreme Court has made its judgment. Some will disagree and others will agree. In the efforts we're making to maintain our Constitutional principles, we will have to abide by what the Supreme Court says. We have a very easy remedy here, and that is to pray ourselves. We can pray a good deal more at home and attend our churches with fidelity and emphasize the true meaning of prayer in the lives of our children. I hope, as a result of that decision, all Americans will give prayer a greater emphasis.[3]

Hearings

A month after *Engel* was handed down, Senator James Oliver Eastland, chairman of the Senate Judiciary Committee, held congressional hearings on the issue of public-school prayer. Surprisingly, much of the attention at the hearings focused not on Justice Hugo Black's majority opinion but on a concurring opinion written by Justice William O. Douglas. Douglas, a colorful character and a consistently liberal, passionate defender of free expression and other civil liberties, was a frequent target of criticism by social conservatives during his many years on the court (1939–1975).

Douglas's concurring opinion in *Engel* opened up a whole new set of possibilities concerning what Douglas viewed as state financing of religion: "The point for decision is whether the Government can constitutionally finance a religious exercise," he wrote. "Our system at the federal and state levels is presently honeycombed

After the Supreme Court's *Engel* decision, President John F. Kennedy encouraged Americans to emphasize prayer in their private lives, rather than fight the Court's ruling.

with such financing. Nevertheless, I think it is an unconstitutional undertaking whatever form it takes."

In other words, Douglas believed that it was inconsistent to outlaw (correctly, in his view) public-school prayer exercises while allowing many other religious exercises in governmental institutions to continue. The argument commonly made to justify these exercises was that they were not so much religious as cultural, part of our national heritage, as a result of having been a part of public life for so long. Douglas did not find this persuasive. His decision clearly spelled out his point of view:

> What New York does on the opening of its public schools is what we do when we open court [with a one-line prayer]. . . . What New York does on the opening of its public schools is what each House of Congress does at the opening of each day's business. . . .
>
> In New York the teacher who leads in prayer is on the public payroll; and the time she takes seems minuscule compared with the salaries appropriated by state legislatures and Congress for chaplains to conduct prayers in the legislative halls. Only a bare fraction of the teacher's time is given to reciting this short 22-word prayer. . . . Yet for me the principle is the same, no matter how briefly the prayer is said, for in each of the instances given the person praying is a public official on the public payroll, performing a religious exercise in a governmental institution. . . .
>
> Once government finances a religious exercise it inserts a divisive influence into our communities. . . . The First Amendment teaches that a government neutral in the field of religion better serves all religious interests.[4]

Some advocates of public-school prayer have argued that many forms of public religious exercise, such as the prayer said by a chaplain at the opening of each day's business in Congress, are American cultural traditions.

Douglas's radical point of view called into question a whole host of long-established government policies that he believed violated the principle of separation of church and state. In a long footnote, Douglas indicated that what he had in mind for banning might include not only chaplains' salaries but also school lunches for students at religious schools, the motto "In God We Trust" stamped on U.S. currency, tax deductions for gifts to charitable religious organizations, and special postal rates for church mailings.

But Douglas's opinion was only a concurring opinion. Unlike the majority opinion in *Engel,* which did not address financing issues, what Douglas wrote was not the law of the land. Nonetheless, many members of Congress seemed concerned that Douglas's opinion might be the direction in which the Supreme Court was heading. Eliminating prayer in public schools today might, they worried, lead to elimination of churches' tax exemptions or other such long-established benefits tomorrow.

Much of the congressional reaction to *Engel,* particularly among white southerners who opposed the civil rights movement, echoed negative reactions to Supreme Court civil rights decisions, particularly *Brown* v. *Board of Education of Topeka.* Many members of Congress objecting to the *Engel* decision did so using the same kind of language as they had used in objecting to *Brown:* The court was abusing its power, intruding into places where it had no business, infringing on "states' rights." Likely in part because of this connection, such civil rights leaders as the Reverend Martin Luther King, Jr., supported *Engel.* King called *Engel* "a sound and good decision reaffirming something that is basic in our Constitution, namely, separation of church and state."[5]

Public Reaction

Official religious reaction to the *Engel* decision was mixed. Officials of the Roman Catholic Church were extremely critical. To the contrary, most Jewish leaders favored the decision. And the reactions of Protestant leaders ranged from strong support to strong condemnation. Leaders of the mainstream, well-established Protestant denominations tended to support or at least go along with the decision, reflecting their general support for separation of church and state. Many fundamentalist Protestants, however, were uncomfortable with the decision. Their concerns were voiced at the grassroots level in their local churches, as well as nationally, by the crusading Reverend Billy Graham and the best-selling inspirational author Norman Vincent Peale.

When the *Schempp* decision banning public school Bible-reading exercises was handed down a year after *Engel,* the immediate reaction was quieter and more moderate. This more moderate and conciliatory tone was particularly evident among clergy, even Catholic clergy.

As with *Engel,* a majority of Americans disapproved of the *Schempp* decision. Fewer, however, seemed inclined to voice their opposition so passionately, even though *Schempp* directly affected far more schools and students than *Engel* did: At the time, thirty-seven states permitted some sort of religious exercises in public schools, with

After the *Engel* decision, grassroots movements like this petition drive were organized to try to restore prayer to public schools.

thirteen states actually requiring Bible reading. *Schempp* declared these exercises unconstitutional.

Perhaps the spoken reaction to *Schempp* was so muted because the decision was so widely disobeyed, especially in southern states. Alabama's Governor George Wallace, for example, defiantly urged: "I would like for the people of Alabama to be in defiance of such a ruling. . . . I want the Supreme Court to know we are not going to conform to any such decision. I want the State Board of Education to tell the whole world we are not going to abide by it."[6]

Elsewhere, many states voided their official laws on school prayer, then quietly looked the other way when local schools, without following any official state policy, continued their prayer exercises. Some state officials erroneously contended that school prayers and Bible readings were constitutional so long as students were not compelled by the state to participate. Most commonly, the interpretation of and obedience to both *Schempp* and *Engel* were left up to local school officials and teachers.

Becker's Crusade

Meanwhile, in Congress, various proposals to amend the Constitution to counter *Engel* and *Schempp* were introduced and discussed. Although Congressman Frank Becker's proposed constitutional amendment after *Engel* had gone nowhere, after *Schempp* was handed down he immediately proposed another. Having already decided to retire from Congress, Becker—a devout Catholic and a strong supporter of public schools—decided to devote himself to a crusade to return religious exercises to public schools.

The proposed constitutional amendment Becker worked out with his colleagues to undo the *Engel* and *Schempp* decisions became known as the "Becker amendment." It read:

> Section 1. Nothing in this Constitution shall be deemed to prohibit the offering, reading from or listening to prayers or Biblical Scriptures, if participation therein is on a voluntary basis, in any governmental or public school, institution, or place.
>
> Section 2. Nothing in this Constitution shall be deemed to prohibit making reference to belief in, reliance upon, or invoking the aid of God or a Supreme Being, in any governmental or public document, proceeding, activity, ceremony, school, institution, or place or upon any coinage, currency, or obligation of the United States.
>
> Section 3. Nothing in this Article shall constitute an establishment of religion.[7]

Congressman Becker's tireless efforts (and his threats to campaign against members of Congress who failed to support his constitutional amendment) eventually persuaded the chairman of the House Judiciary Committee, Emanuel Celler, to hold hearings on the matter in April 1964. "The welfare and entire future of our beloved America depends upon how we handle the most dynamic tradition in our national life—dependence upon Almighty God," Becker said at the start of the hearings. Becker, and those who supported his amendment, repeatedly emphasized that public school prayer should be "voluntary" as well as

Congressman Frank Becker proposed a constitutional amendment that would overturn the *Engel* and *Schempp* decisions, and return religious exercises to American public schools.

"nondenominational" or "nonsectarian" (not tied to any particular religious denomination or sect, such as Presbyterianism, Mormonism, etc.).

Opposition

Many of those who opposed the amendment questioned whether a prayer could be devised that would be both meaningful and truly "nondenominational." For example, one member of the committee, Representative William Cahill of New Jersey, asked Becker and his supporters to "answer specifically three questions as they testify [before the committee]. . . . Who will authorize what prayer, and what Bible? . . . How can we get a prayer that is tolerable to all creeds and preferential to none, and who is going to be the ultimate determining judge as to what prayer is to be used, what version of the Bible is to be used?"[8]

Surprisingly, the most persuasive and articulate testimony against the Becker amendment came from representatives of a wide variety of religious organizations, many of whom objected to the amendment on purely religious grounds. Speaking of the Regents' prayer disallowed by *Engel,* Edwin H. Tuller of the National Council of Churches told the committee, "I live in fear of identifying this with prayer. Because if the children are taught this prayer, then my teaching that prayer is a vital relationship between the individual and his Creator through Jesus Christ is contrary to that teaching."[9] In other words, the Regents' prayer—written by public officials and recited by students not from the heart but because they were told to recite it—wasn't a real prayer at all. To call it a real prayer was an insult and a threat to what Tuller so strongly valued as religion. Speaking more broadly, Tuller said:

> I fear state religion. . . . I feel that if the people of the United States wish to undergird [strengthen] their personal lives and their social life by the power of prayer and Bible reading they have through the free exercise clause not only the right but the responsibility.
>
> The place for this, sir, in my opinion, is in the homes of our country and in the churches and religious institutions. It is not in the public schools. . . . If the public schools are to be used as an agency for evangelism [efforts to change individuals' religious beliefs] or religious education, sir, I think they would tend to weaken rather than strengthen the strong religious witness we have in these United States.
>
> I believe strongly that the strength of our religious heritage among the common people of the United States is posited [set firmly] upon the voluntary nature of such religious conviction; that it would be seriously damaged through any effort of the State to bolster, or strengthen it through these procedures.[10]

Becker's amendment never made it out of committee. It died at the end of the hearings.

The school-prayer issue, however, did not die. Two years later, in August 1966, Congress once again held hearings on the issue, this time in the Senate. In September of that year, the Senate voted down a proposed constitutional amendment favoring "voluntary" school prayer. In 1971, the issue came up yet

Some of the strongest opposition to formal prayer in public schools came from church leaders. Here, a delegation of Maryland religious leaders discusses the issue of school prayer with members of the House of Representatives.

again in the House, which once again failed to approve a school-prayer amendment.

Legislative Efforts

In 1979, Senator Jesse Helms (R-N.C.) introduced an addition to a piece of legislation (not a constitutional amendment) intended to keep the Supreme Court from reviewing any more cases relating to "voluntary prayers in public schools and public buildings." It passed the Senate that year, but not the House. In 1980, amid general doubt that such a legislative effort to tie the hands of the Supreme Court was constitutional (the Justice Department said it wasn't), the House held hearings on the issue. Helms's legislation never made it into law.

The fall 1980 election brought Ronald Reagan to the White House; a Republican majority to the Senate; and a socially conservative religious/political movement of fundamentalist, evangelical Protestants, led by such television preachers as Jerry Falwell and Pat Robertson, to the foreground of national politics. Fostering prayer in public schools was one of a host of social policy issues on the agenda of the religious right and the nation's Republican leadership. And, for the first time since *Engel,* the president of the United States was strongly on their side of the issue.

In May 1982, President Reagan asked the Senate to pass a constitutional amendment favoring prayer in public schools. "Nothing in this Constitution," the amendment read, "shall be construed [interpreted] to prohibit individual or group prayer in public schools or other public institutions. No person shall be required by the United States or by any State to participate in prayer." According to the president, this amendment was to "allow communities to determine for themselves whether prayer should be permitted in their public schools and to allow individuals to decide for themselves whether they wish to participate in prayer."[11]

The Senate held hearings on the president's school prayer amendment in 1982 but took no further action. In the spring of 1983, Senator Helms and Senator Strom Thurmond (R-S.C.) reintroduced the amendment in the Senate. That summer, further hearings were held, at the end of which an additional sentence was added to the proposed amendment: "Neither the United States nor any State shall compose the words of any prayer to be said in public schools."[12] The following spring, the Senate voted against the amendment.

A Moment of Silence

While the school-prayer debate continued off and on in Congress in the 1960s, 1970s, and early 1980s, it played out in schools across the country as well, with various results. Within a few years after *Engel* and *Schempp* were handed down, nearly all of the public schools in the Northeast and along the Pacific coast had complied with the decisions and eliminated Bible reading and prayer exercises from their schools. But in the Midwest and West, many school districts—especially in rural areas—quietly continued religious exercises. In the South, open defiance of the decisions was common.

The state of Alabama had never reconciled itself to

Engel and *Schempp.* Not only did public schools there continue to encourage school prayer but public officials flaunted it. By the early 1980s, the state's school-prayer policy focused on a way it intended to get around some of the objections raised in the *Engel* and *Schempp* cases. Instead of specifying which words students should use to pray with, the state mandated only that a moment of silence be set aside each day for voluntary silent prayer. By 1985, the laws of twenty-five states permitted or provided for such moments of silence in public schools.[13] In *Wallace* v. *Jaffree* (1985), however, the Supreme Court ruled that Alabama's law authorizing a "1-minute period of silence in all public schools 'for meditation or voluntary prayer' . . . is a law respecting the establishment of religion and thus violates the First Amendment."[14]

Ishmael Jaffree, an Alabama resident whose children attended public school, objected to his children's school's practice of having teachers lead their classes in daily prayer. He filed a complaint in court seeking to halt the practice, then filed another, broader complaint against several Alabama statutes concerning public-school prayer. Jaffree and his lawyers contended that such statutes were unconstitutional. As the case worked its way up through the court system to the Supreme Court, it came to focus on one particular issue: whether the moment-of-silence statute passed by Alabama's legislature in 1981 violated the Establishment Clause of the First Amendment.

A decade earlier, in *Lemon* v. *Kurtzman* (1971), the Supreme Court had set forth a three-part test that soon became the standard for determining whether a law is permitted by the Establishment Clause: "First, the statute must have a secular legislative purpose; second, its principal or primary effect must be one that neither advances nor inhibits religion . . . finally, the statute must not foster 'an excessive government entanglement with religion.'"[15] In other words, (1) the law in question must be intended to accomplish some nonreligious, clearly governmental goal; (2) when it takes effect, the law must not first and foremost help or harm religion; and (3) even if it doesn't directly help or harm religion, the law must not cause government to become too involved with religious matters.

Writing for the Supreme Court's majority in *Jaffree*, Justice John Paul Stevens applied the *Lemon* test to the case at hand. Stevens noted that if a law fails to meet the first of the three parts of the *Lemon* test, that alone is enough to disqualify it, without any need even to consider the other two parts of the test. And, according to Stevens, the moment-of-silence statute at issue in *Jaffree* obviously failed that test:

> The record . . . reveals that the enactment of [the Alabama statute] was not motivated by any clearly secular purpose—indeed, the statute had *no* secular purpose.
>
> The sponsor of the bill . . . , [State] Senator Donald Holmes, inserted into the legislative record . . . a statement indicating that the legislation was an "effort to return voluntary prayer" to the public schools. Later Senator Holmes confirmed this purpose before the District Court. In response to the question whether he had any purpose for the legislation other than returning voluntary prayer to public schools, he stated: "No,

I did not have no other purpose in mind." The State
[in defending the statute in court] did not present evidence of any secular purpose.[16]

Stevens concluded that the Alabama state legislature
had adopted the moment-of-prayer statute for the single
purpose of endorsing the essentially religious practice of
prayer. "Such endorsement is not consistent with the
established principle that the government must pursue a
course of complete neutrality toward religion," he noted.
Therefore, he wrote, the Establishment Clause does not
permit it.

The Court left open the possibility that it might find
acceptable some different law providing for a classroom
"moment of silence"—but only if it served some nonreligious purpose beyond simply restoring public-school
prayer. And it was clear that more explicitly religious
vocal prayers were out of the question.

After *Jaffree*, members of Congress supporting
President Reagan's school-prayer amendment continued
to attempt to find some way to push some version of it
toward successful passage. But their numbers and efforts
dwindled. Even before the *Jaffree* decision in 1985, most
congressional attention to religion in public schools had
shifted to a completely different approach: equal access.

5

A New Approach: Equal Access

From the day after the *Engel* decision was handed down through the 1960s, 1970s, and into the 1980s, Congress regularly considered, and rejected, proposed amendments to the U.S. Constitution intended to restore prayer to public schools. In the early 1980s, however, a new alternative emerged, gathered support, and ultimately was enacted into law as the Equal Access Act.

Instead of focusing on the issue of state entanglement with religion, the principle of "equal access" focuses on the First Amendment right of free speech. Instead of arranging for schools to impose religious activities on students (as prior school-prayer amendments would have done), "equal access" addresses which types of restrictions laid on religious activity the schools should lift.

During Senate hearings on President Ronald Reagan's school-prayer amendment in 1982, Senator Mark Hatfield raised the question of allowing students who wished to pray before or after school to have equal access to school facilities. In 1983, the Senate held hearings on the issue. In 1984, the House took up the issue.

One reason for the congressional concern was that some local public-school officials had taken the *Engel* and *Schempp* decisions to mean that public schools must ban any and all forms of religious activity. Ironically, according to some observers, school prayer *supporters* who overstated the reach of the decisions were apparently partly to blame for this. As one witness at a 1983 Senate hearing put it:

> Our problem is this: the Supreme Court's decisions have only invalidated teacher-led, school-initiated, government-sponsored prayer. Now this committee has heard accurate statements from around the country that there are school principals who say, "We cannot allow the Fellowship of Christian Athletes to have a meeting at our school, even though we permit the key club and the rodeo club to meet." There are school principals around the country who think that. Do you know why they think that? They think that, in part, because the President of the United States and many distinguished Members of Congress have for many years been misleading the American people by constantly stating that the U.S. Supreme Court has forbidden all prayer in the public schools. That is just not true.[1]

Equal Access Act

To ensure that high-school students would have the same kind of access to school facilities for religious activities as

After the *Engel* and *Schempp* decisions, many schools felt they were required to ban any activity that might be considered religious. Here, a teacher reads from a book that quotes literary figures, but not Bible passages.

they have for nonreligious activities, Congress in 1984 passed the Equal Access Act. (Although the act would apply equally to students seeking to meet for political discussions and students seeking to meet for prayer, its authors' intent was clearly to ensure an equitable haven for student religious activity in the public schools.) The key clause of the act reads:

> It shall be unlawful for any public secondary school which receives Federal financial assistance and which has a limited open forum to deny equal access or a fair opportunity to, or discriminate against, any students who wish to conduct a meeting within that limited open forum on the basis of the religious, political, philosophical, or other content of the speech at such meetings.[2]

The act defines "limited open forum" as "an offering to or opportunity for one or more non-curriculum related student groups to meet on school premises during noninstructional times." In plainer language, a limited open forum is created when schools allow language clubs, chess teams, and other such voluntary student-interest groups to meet on school property before or after school.

The act's "limited open forum" is thus a limited kind of "public forum" for students in public schools. In American law, the principle of the public forum has come to have a specific meaning: Once a public space is opened to some groups or individuals, government may not prohibit others from using it in a similar manner solely on the basis of the content of their message. (For example, if Republicans and Democrats are allowed to hold political rallies in a public park, other, less popular political parties must be allowed to hold rallies there also.)

High schools may, however, avoid opening up a limited open forum altogether, by simply banning *all* "non-curriculum related student groups." But once a school allows even one such group, it must allow equal access to school facilities for all such groups—or risk being sued for violating the Equal Access Act.

The act goes on to specify in detail what it does and does not obligate schools to do. For example, it specifies that the meetings are to be completely voluntary and student run, they may not be initiated or sponsored by the school, and they may not be directed or even regularly attended by "nonschool persons." Furthermore, the act specifies that it does not authorize any school, or any other government body

(1) to influence the form or content of any prayer or other religious activity;

(2) to require any person to participate in prayer or other religious activity;

(3) to expend public funds beyond the incidental cost of providing the space for student-initiated meetings;

(4) to compel any school agent or employee to attend a school meeting if the content of the speech at the meeting is contrary to the beliefs of the agent or employee;

(5) to sanction meetings that are otherwise unlawful;

63

(6) to limit the rights of groups of students which are not of a specified numerical size; or

(7) to abridge the constitutional rights of any person.[3]

The *Mergens* Case and the Equal Access Act

In June 1990, the U.S. Supreme Court examined the constitutionality of the Equal Access Act in *Board of Education of the Westside Community Schools* v. *Mergens.* In this complicated decision, a majority of the Court's justices agreed that the school district in question had violated the Equal Access Act. However, no such clear majority was willing to agree on reasons why the act itself did not violate the Establishment Clause. Nonetheless, a majority of the justices, for various reasons, chose not to disallow the act. So the Equal Access Act was effectively—though confusingly—affirmed as the law of the land.

At issue in *Mergens* was Westside High School's practice of allowing students to join various student groups sponsored by faculty members and to meet after school hours on school property, while disallowing groups sponsored by political or religious organizations or by any organization discriminating on the basis of race, color, creed, sex, or political belief. A student at the school, Bridget Mergens, sought and was denied permission to form a Christian club under the same rules as other student organizations but without a faculty sponsor. The Christian club was to have been open to any student who wished to participate in its activities—Bible reading and discussion, fellowship, and prayer. Mergens and her supporters took the school district to court to challenge its refusal to allow the Christian club.

Six different religious and civil liberties groups banded together to file a friend-of-the-court brief with the Supreme Court supporting the school district.[4] Their brief argued that the school district's policy on student groups should be upheld and that the Equal Access Act should be declared unconstitutional. They argued that the act and its application in this case "violate the establishment clause of the first amendment; by sanctioning sectarian religious activities in our nation's public schools, it interferes with the right of the individual to believe as he or she sees fit and it undermines the school's ability to instill in students the vital democratic values of respect and tolerance."[5]

On the other side of the dispute, the Rutherford Institute (a public policy law firm concerned with religious issues) filed a friend-of-the-court brief supporting Bridget Mergens. Their brief argued that disallowing Mergens's Christian club was "inconsistent with our nation's commitment to free speech and religious freedom." They asserted that both the Equal Access Act and the U.S. Constitution protect such religion-oriented student groups from being excluded from access to school facilities allowed to other student groups. But not only should the court allow Mergens's group to meet, the brief continued, it should also take this opportunity to affirm that the Equal Access Act is constitutional. "The Equal Access Act is perfectly consistent with the Establishment Clause and this Court's prior decisions," they wrote. And regardless, the brief continued, the school district's "policy of censoring the private religious speech of students violates the Establishment, Free Speech, and Free Exercise Clauses" of the First Amendment.[6] (The clauses referred to here are: "Congress shall make no law respecting an establishment of religion; or prohibiting the free exercise thereof; or abridging the freedom of speech. . . .")

Justice Sandra Day O'Connor wrote the opinion for the majority of the Supreme Court, concluding that the school district had "violated the Equal Access Act by denying official recognition to [Mergens's] proposed club." O'Connor compared the situation at the school with the requirements of the act in some detail, and found that:

> Westside's denial of [Mergens's] request to form a religious group constitutes a denial of "equal access" to the school's limited open forum. Although the school apparently permits [Mergens and her fellow students] to meet informally after school, they seek equal access in the form of official recognition, which allows clubs to be part of the student activities program and carries with it access to the school newspaper, bulletin boards, public address system, and annual Club Fair. Since denial of such recognition is based on the religious content of the meetings [Mergens and her fellow students] wish to conduct within the school's limited open forum, it violates the Act.[7]

On the issue of whether the Equal Access Act was constitutional, however, the Court could not muster a

Justice Sandra Day O'Connor delivered a majority opinion for the Supreme Court in the *Mergens* case, saying that preventing the formation of a religious club in a public school was a violation of the Equal Access Act.

simple majority opinion. Even though a majority of the justices agreed that the act was constitutional, they could not agree on the reasons why. Writing for only four of the Court's nine justices, O'Connor applied the Lemon test to the act and found that it passed. (The act (1) served a secular purpose, (2) did not have the primary effect of advancing or inhibiting religion, and (3) did not excessively entangle the state with religion.)

Two other justices, Anthony Kennedy and Antonin Scalia, agreed that the act was constitutional but not on the grounds of the *Lemon* test. Instead, they emphasized that, under the act, the government did not either "give direct benefits to religion in such a degree that it in fact establishes a state religion or religious faith, or tends to do so" or "coerce any student to participate in a religious activity." These reasons alone, they argued, were sufficient to uphold the act's constitutionality.[8]

Two more justices, Thurgood Marshall and William Brennan, were more uneasy about the act's implications for separation of church and state. While "agreeing that the Act as applied to Westside *could* withstand Establishment Clause scrutiny," they also concluded that "the inclusion of the Christian club in the type of forum presently established at the school . . . will not assure government neutrality toward religion. . . . Westside must take steps to fully disassociate itself from the Christian club's religious speech and avoid appearing to sponsor or endorse the club's goals."[9]

So, while eight of the Court's nine justices (Justice John Paul Stevens dissented) agreed that the Equal Access Act was constitutional in at least some circumstances, they came to their conclusions for very different and not entirely compatible reasons. However, recent changes in Court personnel make it probable that the Court is moving toward a majority that agrees with Justice O'Connor's approach to the act. Meanwhile, although the Establishment Clause issues raised by the act have not been definitively decided, the act remains the law of the land, and local high schools are obliged to obey it.

The Religious Freedom Restoration Act

In 1993, Congress further complicated the Equal Access Act picture when it passed the Religious Freedom Restoration Act (RFRA). RFRA requires that the government may not "substantially burden a person's exercise of religion" unless it demonstrates that the burden in question both furthers a compelling governmental interest, such as public safety, and is the least restrictive way to accomplish that interest. For example, the state may prosecute as child abusers parents who refuse to allow their children needed medical care for religious reasons. If, however, adequate medical care can be provided in a way that meets the parents' religious requirements, the state may not insist that the parents choose a kind of care not allowed by their religion.

Although Congress specified that RFRA should not be "construed to affect, interpret, or in any way address that portion of the First Amendment prohibiting laws respecting the establishment of religion," it nonetheless seems likely that the act will figure in future challenges to restrictions on public school prayer. According to the

National School Board Association's Council of School Attorneys:

> Students may attempt to use RFRA to get prayer in school or at school-sponsored activities. Although in some limited situations schools may be required under free speech principles to allow students to engage in private prayer, such as on the playground during lunch or recess, it is exceedingly doubtful that a RFRA claim would be upheld in any situation because of the option students have to pray silently in school or aloud in non-school locations.[10]

6

Public School Prayer
in the 1990s

Three decades after *Engel* v. *Vitale* (1962), public school prayer remained an open issue. It was clear that the Supreme Court considered formal prayer and Bible reading unconstitutional as regular parts of the public-school day. But what about prayer on special occasions, where attendance is voluntary, such as at graduation ceremonies?

Nearly thirty years to the day after *Engel* was handed down, on June 24, 1992, the Supreme Court ruled in *Lee* v. *Weisman* that "including clergy who offer prayers as part of an official public school graduation ceremony is forbidden by the Establishment Clause."[1] Even after two successive presidents (Ronald Reagan and George Bush) who favored school prayer had made five Supreme Court appointments over twelve years, the Court still held to the basic principles set forth in *Engel* and *Schempp*.

Lee v. *Weisman*

The *Lee* v. *Weisman* case arose when Daniel Weisman, the father of Deborah Weisman, a student at a public school in Rhode Island, objected to the inclusion of any prayers at his daughter's middle-school graduation ceremony. At the invitation of the school's principal, a rabbi presented opening and closing prayers at Deborah's 1989 graduation. (The choice of a rabbi was apparently intended to placate Mr. Weisman, who had previously complained about the explicitly Christian prayers offered at an older daughter's graduation by a Baptist minister. The Weismans are Jewish.) Afterward, Mr. Weisman sought through court action to have such prayers banned at future graduations, including Deborah's high-school graduation.

Writing for the Supreme Court's majority, Justice Anthony Kennedy noted that:

> The Establishment Clause was inspired by the lesson that in the hands of government what might begin as a tolerant expression of religious views may end in a policy to indoctrinate and coerce. Prayer exercises in elementary and secondary schools carry a particular risk of indirect coercion. . . . The school district's supervision and control of a high school graduation ceremony places subtle and indirect public and peer pressure on attending students to stand as a group or maintain respectful silence during the invocation and benediction [opening and closing prayers].[2]

Not only were students pressured to participate in the prayers if they attended the graduation ceremony, but also students felt pressured to attend the ceremony in the first place, even though they could receive their diplomas

72

without doing so. "In this society," Justice Kennedy observed, "high school graduation is one of life's most significant occasions, and a student is not free to absent herself from the exercise in any real sense of the term 'voluntary.'"[3]

Justice Kennedy emphasized that:

The government involvement with religious activity in this case is pervasive, to the point of creating a state-sponsored and state-directed religious exercise in a public school. . . . It is beyond dispute that, at a minimum, the Constitution guarantees that government may not coerce anyone to support or participate in religion or its exercise, or otherwise act in a way which "establishes a [state] religion or religious faith or tends to do so. . . ." The State's involvement in the school prayers challenged today violates these central principles.[4]

In this case, Justice Kennedy continued,

a school official, the principal, decided that an invocation and a benediction should be given. . . . The principal chose the religious participant, here a rabbi. . . . Principal Lee provided Rabbi Gutterman with a copy of the "Guidelines for Civic Occasions" [a pamphlet dealing with prayer at such events prepared by the National Conference of Christians and Jews], and advised him that his prayers should be nonsectarian [not distinctive of a particular religious group]. Through these means the principal directed and controlled the content of the prayer.

Kennedy had noted earlier in his opinion that "the directions may have been given in a good faith attempt to make the prayers acceptable to most persons does not resolve the dilemma caused by the school's involvement."[5]

According to Justice Kennedy,

[t]he First Amendment's Religion Clauses mean that religious beliefs and religious expression are too precious to be either proscribed or prescribed [forbidden or dictated] by the State. . . . All creeds must be tolerated and none favored. . . . The lessons of the First Amendment are as urgent in the modern world as in the 18th Century when it was written. One timeless lesson is that if citizens are subjected to state-sponsored religious exercises, the State disavows its own duty to guard and respect that sphere of inviolable conscience and belief which is the mark of a free people.[6]

Justice Kennedy specifically rejected the argument that such short and unobjectionable prayers didn't matter very much one way or another. Surely the prayers mattered to at least some of those present, and to believe that they didn't "would be an affront to the Rabbi who offered them and to all those for whom the prayers were an essential and profound recognition of divine authority."[7]

In his concluding paragraph, Justice Kennedy touched upon the kinds of concerns that the Equal Access Act addressed,

Our society would be less than true to its heritage if it lacked abiding concern for the values of its young people and we acknowledge the profound belief of adherents to many faiths that there must be a place in the student's life for precepts of a morality higher even than the law we today enforce. We express no

74

hostility to those aspirations. . . . A relentless and pervasive attempt to exclude religion from every aspect of public life could itself become inconsistent with the Constitution.[8]

Citing *Mergens,* the Equal Access Act's test case, he continued:

> We recognize that, at graduation time and throughout the course of the educational process, there will be instances when religious values, religious practices, and religious persons will have some inter-action with the public schools and their students. . . . But these matters, often questions of accommodation of religion, are not before us. The sole question presented [in *Weisman*] is whether a religious exercise may be conducted at a graduation ceremony in circumstances where, as we have found, young graduates who object are induced to conform. No holding by this Court suggests that a school can persuade or compel a student to participate in a religious exercise. That is being done here, and it is forbidden by the Establishment Clause of the First Amendment.[9]

Student-Led Prayer

Only a year later, however, in June 1993, the Supreme Court let stand (approved without writing a detailed opinion of its own) a federal appeals court ruling allowing student-led prayer at graduations. In this case, *Jones* v. *Clear Creek Independent School District,* the school district allowed high-school seniors to vote on whether or not to include a "nonsectarian and non-proselytizing" prayer, to be written and delivered by a

More than three decades after the *Engel* and *Schempp* decisions were delivered, the issue of prayer in public schools is still being challenged in the Supreme Court.

student volunteer, at their graduation ceremony. In upholding the practice, the appeals court wrote that student-led graduation prayers

> place less psychological pressure on students than the prayers at issue in *Lee* because all students, *after having participated in the decision of whether prayers will be given,* are aware that any prayers represent the will of their peers, who are less able to coerce participation than an authority figure from the state or clergy.[10]

After *Jones,* school officials across the country received dozens of requests for student-led prayers at graduations. An organization established by religious right activist Pat Robertson sent letters to fifteen thousand high schools encouraging them to include student-led prayer at graduations.[11] Lawyers for organizations favoring, and for those opposing, public-school prayer offered to support students on either side of the issue.

Jones has thus created a thorny problem for public school administrators seeking to avoid school-prayer lawsuits. Lawyers for the National School Board Association in 1994 offered the following advice:

> The controversy surrounding student-led prayer at public school commencement exercises is very much alive. . . . Public school officials have four options concerning graduation ceremonies: (1) a ceremony including a student-led prayer, invocation or benediction; (2) a ceremony including a moment of silence; (3) a ceremony without prayer, invocation or benediction; or (4) no graduation ceremony.[12]

In at least some schools, the issue of formal prayer

exercises as a part of the regular school day continues to be contested. One widely publicized controversy of this kind has played out in Jackson, Mississippi.

Prayer and Public Address Systems

In November 1993, a Jackson, Mississippi, high-school principal named Bishop Knox was dismissed from his job for allowing students on three separate occasions to recite a brief prayer over the school's public address system. "A group of students went to Dr. Knox with the idea," Kim Fail, president of the school's student body, later recalled. "He, in turn, turned it over to the student council, and we voted on the idea. We thought it was a good idea, so we turned it over to the entire student body to vote on." The vote was 490 to 96 in favor of the idea.[13] (About three hundred students didn't vote.)[14]

Principal Knox decided, based on *Jones,* that such a prayer would be constitutional, and he allowed the students to go ahead with it. "I think that good behavior has to be taught," he later said, "and it has to have a foundation by which it can be taught, and I do believe that to acknowledge God would provide that foundation."[15]

Ms. Fail recited the following prayer amid other daily announcements over the public address system: "Almighty God, we ask Your blessings on our parents, our teachers, and our country throughout the day. In Your name we pray, Amen." As a result, Principal Knox was suspended from his job pending an investigation of the matter.[16] The school superintendent cited *Engel* to justify the suspension.

Students, parents, and other concerned citizens

protested the school district's treatment of Knox. Thousands of his supporters demonstrated at the state capital. The controversy attracted national attention.

In April 1994, a county court ordered that Knox be given his job back, after the governor of Mississippi, earlier that month, signed a law allowing student-led prayer in the state's public schools. In December 1994, however, in a separate case, a federal court in Mississippi declared that law unconstitutional.[17] The court reaffirmed that only at such special events as graduations, not as a regular classroom exercise, was student-led prayer constitutionally acceptable.

School Prayer in Practice

Across the country, public schools in the 1990s have pursued a wide variety of policies on prayer, ranging from vocal classroom prayer in direct defiance of *Engel* and *Schempp* to overly rigid restriction of even constitutionally protected religious activity in the schools. For example, in testimony before a congressional subcommittee in 1995 an attorney specializing in religious liberty cases cited several incidents that he said had taken place since the Equal Access Act became law:

> Notwithstanding the Equal Access Act, student-initiated Bible clubs on public school campuses are still frequent targets of discrimination.
>
> For example, schools have allowed secular clubs to meet during the day but require the religious clubs to meet only after school hours, which results in low attendance at these clubs because of the inconvenient meeting times.
>
> Other schools have allowed students to have

79

Despite the Supreme Court's rulings, some public schools have quietly continued to have teachers and students lead classes in reciting prayers or reading Bible passages, while other schools have allowed a moment of silence at the start of the school day.

secular clubs pictured in the annual while barring the religious clubs. Alternatively, schools have allowed secular clubs access to bulletin boards while still censoring access to the board by the religious or pro-life clubs.[18]

More than thirty years after *Engel,* local disputes concerning school prayer continue to arise. Many are taken to court, with mixed results.

Opposing Viewpoints

School-prayer advocates claim that the Supreme Court has banished God from the public schools. According to conservative activist Phyllis Schlafly,

> [the] right to pray in public schools . . . was taken away from the American people by the U.S. Supreme Court 20 years ago. . . . The U.S. Supreme Court overturned centuries of law, custom, tradition, and educational practice when it censored prayer and Bible reading out of the public schools. The Court simply rewrote the First Amendment in *Engel* v. *Vitale* (1962) and *Abington* v. *Schempp* (1963) to require an absolutist banning of religion that could not be justified by the text of the Constitution, the intent of the Founding Fathers, or American history.[19]

To the contrary, civil liberties groups such as People for the American Way contend:

> In fact, the Supreme Court has not expelled God, Bible reading, or prayer from public schools. . . .
>
> Students have always been free to pray on their own in public schools, subject to the time, place and manner requirements placed on all other forms

of expression. They must express their faith in a non-disruptive fashion. . . . A student, for instance, cannot get up in the middle of class and sing a hymn, just as he or she cannot get up in the middle of class and sing the National Anthem.

Individual students may pray silently any time during the school day, including class. They have opportunities to pray vocally and in groups at lunch, before and after school, and during other free time.[20]

Many religious groups, as well, strongly oppose any form of school prayer that can be construed as state-sanctioned prayer. For them, it is a religious issue as well as a civil liberties issue: They believe that prayer is too important and too deeply personal a matter to be given over to government. For example, representatives of Quakers (members of a Protestant sect that strongly emphasizes individual conscience), in 1995 testimony before a congressional subcommittee, noted that:

The genius of the United States is that it protects—through its congressional and legal systems—the right of each ethnic and religious group to define itself and to speak in its own voice.

For a religious group that wishes to speak in its own voice, there is no time more precious than the time of prayer. No public process or public employee should define that time, or suggest the voice that will speak the prayer, or offer the words that will be prayed. The time of prayer is a time defined only by the person and the spirit with whom he or she communicates.

We wish to emphasize that we favor prayer. For many of us in this room—Quakers and others—our

82

own spiritual journeys and our relationships with God, or the Spirit of Christ, or the Light Within, as we may variously express it, are central to our daily lives. Because of the importance of prayer, and because we value the development of our own spiritual journeys and those of our children, we ask this Committee to forego any notion that prayer can or should be "taught" in the public schools. Prayer is not taught—it grows within a faith community, nurtured by the teachings of elders in that faith and sustained by the explorations of children and seekers.

We oppose prayers organized and led by the public schools as institutions, and by teachers as public employees.[21]

The Supreme Court since *Weisman* has indicated that it may be reluctant to reopen and clarify the issue of public school prayer. It refused to take on the *Jones* case. More recently, for months through the spring of 1995, the Court sat in silence concerning a challenge to an Idaho school district's policy allowing student-led prayer at graduation. In June, after the student bringing suit graduated, the Court declared the case moot (no longer a valid case since the graduation at issue had already taken place), leaving the issues that opened up the case in the first place unresolved. *Lee* v. *Weisman,* the Court's most recent school prayer decision, had generated bitter debate among the justices. Perhaps they didn't wish to revisit the issue until a clearer consensus emerged from the lower courts or among the Supreme Court justices themselves.

With the Supreme Court standing back, the main national arena for the school prayer issue shifted to Congress.

83

7

Voices Shaping National Policy in the 1990s

In November 1994, voters swept a Republican majority into both houses of Congress with an agenda strongly favoring public school prayer. Just before the election, Republican leader Newt Gingrich (soon to be the new speaker of the House of Representatives) said:

> This country is on the edge of historic victories. And I believe that school prayer will be one of the seminal fights of the decade. School prayer is important in itself because we should have the right to pray voluntarily in school—and to have student-led prayers. More importantly, that right makes America unique as a civilization—and establishes the battleground for America's future.[1]

The Contract with America

School prayer was not featured in the "Contract With America," the Republican campaign document coauthored by Gingrich and released in the last days of the 1994 congressional election campaigns, which spelled out ten changes that the Republicans promised to bring up for voting during the first one hundred days of the 104th Congress. Nonetheless, within days of the Republicans' victory, Gingrich and other Republican leaders announced that they would hold nationwide hearings on a constitutional amendment favoring public-school prayer.

In reaction, President Clinton indicated that he was willing to discuss the issue, and later clarified that what he had in mind was a wordless "moment of reflection." However, the idea of holding school-prayer hearings was soon criticized at a meeting of the nation's governors as a distraction from Congress's more urgent business. "If we don't deal with the economic issues," Michigan Governor John Engler said, "we'll need more than prayer to solve our problems."[2]

And, in fact, Congress did concentrate in the early months of 1995 on such "Contract" issues as balancing the federal budget, reforming welfare, and revising the crime bill passed in 1994. It did not hold any school-prayer hearings, nor did it tackle other contentious social issues such as abortion.

The politically active religious right grew impatient. While they supported the Republicans' economic agenda, that wasn't the chief reason why so many of them had voted Republican in 1994. They longed for action on a conservative social agenda featuring strong support for public-school prayer. Socially conservative Republicans who had put that agenda on hold while Congress

Republican leader Newt Gingrich (right) led a call for a constitutional amendment favoring prayer in public schools. In response, President Bill Clinton (center) said he might be willing to consider a "moment of reflection."

acted on the "Contract With America" began to press for congressional action after the spring 1995 recess.

The Christian Coalition

In May, the Christian Coalition, a powerful conservative lobbying group that had strongly supported the Republicans in the 1994 elections, issued a ten-point "Contract With the American Family," which it called a "blueprint" for social reform legislation. The Christian Coalition's "contract" included calls for restricting abortion, abolishing the federal Department of Education, and turning welfare over to private charities. Its very first point called for a constitutional amendment on school prayer:

Religious Equality

Passage of the Religious Equality Amendment to protect the religious liberties of Americans in public places.

The amendment would not restore compulsory, sectarian prayer or Bible-reading dictated by government officials. We seek a balanced approach that allows voluntary, student- and citizen-initiated free speech in non-compulsory settings such as courthouse lawns, high school graduation ceremonies, and sports events.[3]

In an expanded, book-length version of the "Contract," the Christian Coalition explained why it felt such an amendment was needed:

With each passing year, people of faith grow increasingly distressed by the hostility of public institutions toward religious expression. We have

87

witnessed the steady erosion of the time-honored rights of religious Americans—both as individuals and as communities—to practice what they believe in the public square. This erosion has been abetted by a court system which stands the plain meaning of the First Amendment on its head. The time has now come to amend the Constitution to restore freedom of speech for America's people of faith.[4]

Speaker of the House Newt Gingrich promised to bring legislation based on the Christian Coalition's "Contract" up for voting in the House of Representatives.

School-Prayer Guidelines

Soon thereafter, in July 1995, President Clinton sent to Attorney General Janet Reno and Secretary of Education Richard Riley a set of guidelines to govern religious expression in public schools, including school prayer. The guidelines (which had clearly been shaped by "Religion in the Public Schools: A Joint Statement of Current Law," a pamphlet issued in April 1995 by a coalition of religious and civil liberties organizations) specified that students could voluntarily engage in group prayer so long as they did not compel others to join them. In his memorandum to Ms. Reno and Mr. Riley, the president elaborated:

Nothing in the First Amendment converts our public schools into religion-free zones, or requires all religious expression to be left behind at the schoolhouse door. While the government may not use schools to coerce the conscience of our students or to convey official endorsement of religion, the government's schools also may not discriminate against private religious expression during the school day. . . .

The First Amendment permits—and protects—a greater degree of religious expression in public schools than many Americans may now understand. . . . The following principles are among those that apply to religious expression in our schools:

. . . The Establishment Clause of the First Amendment does not prohibit purely private religious speech by students. Students therefore have the same right to engage in individual or group prayer and religious discussion during the school day as they do to engage in other comparable activity. For example, students may read their Bibles or other scriptures, say grace before meals, and pray before tests to the same extent they may engage in comparable nondisruptive activities. Local school authorities possess substantial discretion to impose rules of order and other pedagogical [teaching-related] restrictions on student activities, but they may not discriminate against religious activity or speech.[5]

By the time the president issued these guidelines, the 1996 presidential campaign was already under way. Predictably, most of the Republican contenders favored school prayer. According to front-runner Bob Dole's campaign organization: "Throughout his career, Bob Dole has been a strong and consistent supporter of student-led voluntary school prayer. His support goes back as far as 1967 when he first supported a voluntary prayer amendment to the Constitution." In the spring of 1995, candidate Pat Buchanan expressed his point of view in colorful and fiery rhetoric:

In July 1995, President Bill Clinton issued a set of guidelines on religious matters in public schools, including school prayer.

When many of us were young, public schools and Catholic schools, Christian schools and Jewish schools, instructed children in their religious heritage and Judeo-Christian values, in what was right and what was wrong. We were taught about the greatness and goodness of this land we call God's country, in which we are all so fortunate to live. . . .

But today, in too many of our schools our children are being robbed of their innocence. Their minds are being poisoned against their Judeo-Christian heritage, against America's heroes and against American history, against the values of faith and family and country.

Eternal truths that do not change from the Old and New Testament have been expelled from our public schools, and our children are being indoctrinated in moral relativism, and the propaganda of an anti-Western ideology.

Parents everywhere are fighting for their children. And to the mothers and fathers waging those battles, let me say: This campaign is your campaign. Your fight is our fight.[6]

Constitutional Amendments

Just as the presidential race was beginning to heat up, not one but two constitutional amendments pertaining to school prayer were introduced in Congress, in November 1995. The first, known as the Religious Equality Amendment, introduced by Representative Henry Hyde (R-Ill.), read: "Neither the United States nor any state shall deny benefits to or otherwise discriminate against any private person or group on account of religious

91

expression, belief, or identity; nor shall the prohibition on laws respecting an establishment of religion be construed to require such discrimination." Senator Orrin Hatch (R-Utah) introduced a comparable amendment in the Senate. Although the amendment did not mention school prayer directly, its prohibition of discrimination against the expression of religious views—of which prayer is but one form—would include public schools as well as other public venues, such as public radio stations.

The other amendment, introduced by Representative Ernest J. Istook, Jr. (R-Okla.), and known as the Istook amendment, did specifically target school prayer:

> To secure the people's right to acknowledge God according to the dictates of conscience: Nothing in this Constitution shall prohibit acknowledgments of the religious heritage, beliefs, or traditions of the people, or prohibit student-sponsored prayer in public schools. Neither the United States nor any State shall compose any official prayer or compel joining in prayer, or discriminate against religious expression or belief.[7]

Both amendments were widely criticized by religious and civil liberties groups favoring strict separation of church and state. Speaking of the Religious Equality Amendment, People for the American Way warned:

> In an effort to mobilize support for their radical proposal, amendment backers commonly distort its impact, . . . describing it as an attempt to secure the religious liberty of students and citizens in general. The amendment would, in fact, foster state-sponsored prayer and even outright proselytization [attempts to change the religious beliefs] of captive

audiences in schoolrooms, military barracks, courtrooms and other public areas—the very type of religious coercion the First Amendment prohibits. . . .

Religious Right leaders and their political leaders have sought for some time to use the machinery of the state to promote prayer in the classroom under circumstances controlled by school teachers or by other government officials. The "Religious Equality Amendment" is the capstone of that effort.[8]

According to the Coalition to Preserve Religious Liberty, the Hyde/Hatch amendments were

mostly about money. They would radically alter the First Amendment by requiring the government to subsidize pervasively sectarian entities (including churches, synagogues and parochial schools) to the same extent it subsidizes secular entities. They would threaten our religious liberty by upsetting the delicate balance of church-state relations. This balance has provided an unparalleled degree of protection for faiths of all kinds for over two centuries. The amendments should be rejected by Congress and the American people.[9]

On the other hand, the amendments also had many supporters. The Christian Coalition, which strongly supported the Religious Equality Amendment in its "Contract With the American Family," declared:

It is time for people of faith in America to restore the right to freedom of religious expression. It is time to illuminate the meaning of the First Amendment and the fundamental liberties it offers to all of [its] citizens. It is time to reclaim for religious expression the free speech protections it never should have lost.

Some may argue that extending First Amendment rights to such religious expression as voluntary, student-initiated prayer by a high school valedictorian at a graduation ceremony is somehow "coercive."

Others may object that a Religious Equality Amendment will simply establish a state religion by the back door. It will have the opposite effect. By forcing the government to expel all religious expression from the public sphere, the current judicial interpretation has marginalized [sidelined] faith in our public life. A Religious Equality Amendment will simply restore the free-speech rights of religious Americans to equality with those already enjoyed by their nonreligious fellow citizens.[10]

The Istook amendment drew fire from the same organizations as the Religious Equality Amendment. "Rep. Istook's proposal will allow for religious coercion in our public schools and authorize government misuse of religion for political ends," the Coalition to Preserve Religious Liberty said. "It will also invite greater government intrusion into our private religious lives and create greater confusion about the proper boundaries between church and state. Finally . . . it could open the door to government funding of parochial schools [run by religious organizations] and the ministries of sectarian religious groups. It should be rejected by Congress and the American people."[11]

To the contrary, Representative Istook says in defense of his amendment:

The Religious Liberties Amendment . . . was introduced to reverse trends of suppressing religious expression. . . .

To continue the intentions of our Founding Fathers, the Religious Liberties Amendment provides a limited government approach to protecting religious freedom. Separation of church and state does not mean regulation by the state or the judicial court system. The authors of the Constitution intended to protect religious freedom.

The Religious Liberties Amendment would allow student-sponsored prayer in public schools, but it does not enforce any official prayer in schools or require students to join in prayer. . . .

The Religious Liberties Amendment restores the original intent of the First Amendment to protect the religious freedom of the American people.[12]

After President Bill Clinton's reelection to office in the fall of 1996, lawmakers set the school-prayer issue aside while they worked on other issues. But many lawmakers still had strong feelings about school prayer. In addition, various school-prayer-related lawsuits were still heading for the U.S. Supreme Court. The United States was too far from any common ground on this issue for anyone to expect it to be resolved anytime soon.

Chapter Notes

Chapter 1

1. *School District of Abington Township, Pennsylvania, et al. v. Schempp et al.,* 374 U.S. 203.

2. Quoted in Robert S. Alley, *School Prayer: The Court, the Congress, and the First Amendment* (Buffalo, N.Y.: Prometheus Books, 1994), p. 124.

3. Ibid., pp. 122–123.

4. National Public Radio, "Morning Edition," January 25, 1994.

5. Speech delivered by Newt Gingrich at the Heritage Foundation on October 5, 1994, reprinted in *Family Voice,* March 1995.

6. Speech delivered on July 12, 1995, at James Madison High School, Vienna, Va., transcript provided by the White House.

Chapter 2

1. John Locke's "Letter Concerning Toleration," quoted in Leo Pfeffer, *Church, State, and Freedom,* rev. ed. (Boston: Beacon Press, 1967), p. 102.

2. Ibid., p. 133.

3. Ibid., p. 125.

4. Ibid., p. 327.

5. Howard M. Squadron's testimony on behalf of American Jewish Congress at a House subcommittee hearing held in New York on July 10, 1995, transcript supplied by American Jewish Congress.

6. ACLU Briefing Paper Number 3: "Church and State," undated, supplied to author by ACLU.

Chapter 3

1. *Engel et al. v. Vitale et al.,* 370 U.S. 421.

2. Ibid.

3. Petitioners' brief for the Supreme Court in *Engel v. Vitale.*

4. Ibid.

5. Respondents' brief for the Supreme Court in *Engel v. Vitale.*

6. Ibid.

7. *Engel v. Vitale.*

8. Ibid.

9. Ibid.

10. Ibid.

11. Ibid.

12. *School District of Abington Township, Pennsylvania, et al. v. Schempp et al.,* 374 U.S. 203.

13. Ibid.

14. Ibid.

15. Murrays' petition, quoted in *Abington v. Schempp.*

16. Plaintiffs' brief for the Supreme Court in *Abington v. Schempp.*

17. School officials' brief for the Supreme Court in *Abington v. Schempp.*

18. *Abington v. Schempp.*

19. Ibid.

20. Ibid.

Chapter 4

1. Cited in William M. Beaney and Edward N. Beiser, "Prayer and Politics: The Impact of *Engel* and *Schempp* on the Political Process," *Journal of Public Law,* 13, 1964, pp. 478–479, reprinted in Robert Sikorski, *Prayer in Public Schools and the U.S. Constitution 1961–1992,* (New York:

Garland Publishing, 1993), vol. 1, *Government-Sponsored Religious Activities in Public Schools and the Constitution*, pp. 414–415.

2. Both congressmen quoted in Robert S. Alley, *School Prayer: The Court, the Congress, and the First Amendment* (Buffalo, N.Y.: Prometheus Books, 1994), p. 109.

3. In Beaney and Beiser, p. 416.

4. Concurring opinion of Justice William O. Douglas in *Engel et al.* v. *Vitale et al.* 370 U.S. 421.

5. In Beaney and Beiser, p. 418.

6. Ibid., p. 422.

7. H.J. Res. 693, 88th Congress, quoted in Leo Pfeffer, *Church, State, and Freedom*, rev. ed. (Boston: Beacon Press, 1967), p. 477.

8. In Alley, p. 132.

9. Ibid., p. 141.

10. Ibid., p. 153.

11. Ibid., pp. 197, 199.

12. Ibid., p. 202.

13. Justice Sandra Day O'Connor's concurring opinion in *Wallace, Governor of Alabama, et al.* v. *Jaffree et al.*, 472 U.S. 38.

14. *Wallace* v. *Jaffree.*

15. *Lemon* v. *Kurtzman*, 403 U.S. 602, quoted in *Wallace* v. *Jaffree.*

16. *Wallace* v. *Jaffree.*

Chapter 5

1. Professor Walter Dellinger, of Duke University, quoted in Robert S. Alley, *School Prayer: The Court, the Congress, and the First Amendment* (Buffalo, N.Y.: Prometheus Books, 1994), pp. 202–203.

2. Equal Access Act, reprinted in National School Board Association, *Religion, Education, and the U.S. Constitution* (Alexandria, Va.: NSBA, 1994), pp. 178–179.

3. Ibid.

4. The groups were: Anti-Defamation League of B'nai B'rith, American Civil Liberties Union, National Coalition for Public Education and Religious Liberty, National Jewish Community Relations Advisory Council, Committee for Public Education and Religious Liberty, and Americans for Religious Liberty.

5. Amicus brief in *Board of Education of the Westside Community Schools* v. *Mergens*, 496 U.S. 226.

6. Ibid.

7. Syllabus for *Mergens*.

8. Ibid.

9. Ibid.

10. Both the excerpts from RFRA and the attorneys' advice are from *Religion, Education, and the U.S. Constitution*, pp. 176–177 and p. 155, respectively.

Chapter 6

1. *Robert E. Lee, Individually and as Principal of Nathan Bishop Middle School, et al., Petitioners* v. *Daniel Weisman, etc.,* 112 U.S. 2649.

2. Ibid.

3. Ibid.

4. Ibid.

5. Ibid.

6. Ibid.

7. Ibid.

8. Ibid.

9. Ibid.

10. Fifth Circuit Court of Appeals decision in *Jones* v. *Clear Creek Independent School District,* quoted in National School Board Association, *Religion, Education, and the U.S. Constitution* (Alexandria, Va.: NSBA, 1994), p. 63, emphasis in original.

11. ABC's "World News Tonight," June 4, 1993.

12. *Religion, Education, and the U.S. Constitution,* p. 64.

13. "Larry King Live," CNN, December. 3, 1993.

14. National Public Radio, "Morning Edition," January 25, 1994.

15. Ibid.

16. "Larry King Live."

17. *Facts on File,* December 31, 1994, p. 991.

18. Mathew Staver, president of Liberty Counsel, testifying before the House Judiciary Subcommittee on the Constitution Field Hearing in Tampa, Fla., on June 23, 1995, transcript provided by Liberty Counsel.

19. Phyllis Schlafly, "Prayer in Public Schools," *The Phyllis Schlafly Report,* July 1982.

20. People for the American Way, "The 'Religious Coercion' Amendment: Trampling Religious Liberty in the Name of Religion," with cover letter dated August 22, 1995.

21. "Quakers Urge Government to Stay Out of Private Prayer," press release dated June 11, 1995, from Friends Committee on National Legislation.

Chapter 7

1. Speech delivered by Newt Gingrich at the Heritage Foundation on October 5, 1994, reprinted in *Family Voice,* March 1995.

2. *Facts on File,* December 1, 1994, p. 893.

3. Christian Coalition, press release summarizing their "Contract With the American Family," issued May 17, 1995, reprinted in *Facts on File,* September 28, 1995, p. 715.

4. Christian Coalition, *Contract With the American Family* (Nashville, Tenn.: Moorings, 1995), p. 1.

5. "Text of President Clinton's Memorandum on Religion in Schools," *The New York Times,* July 13, 1995.

6. Announcement speech by Pat Buchanan, when he formally entered the 1996 presidential race, delivered in New Hampshire on March 20, 1995, transcript downloaded from Buchanan campaign's World Wide Web site March 1996.

7. "Religious Liberties Amendment: Talking Points," supplied by Representative Istook's Washington office (undated).

8. People for the American Way, "The 'Religious Coercion' Amendment: Trampling Religious Liberty in the Name of Religion," with cover letter dated August 22, 1995.

9. Coalition to Preserve Religious Liberty, "Talking Points on Rep. Hyde's and Sen. Hatch's 'Religious Equality' Constitutional Amendments," undated, provided to author by Baptist Joint Committee on Public Affairs.

10. Christian Coalition, *Contract With the American Family,* pp. 9–10.

11. Coalition to Preserve Religious Liberty, "Talking Points on Rep. Istook's 'Religious Liberties' Constitutional Amendment," undated, provided to author by Baptist Joint Committee on Public Affairs.

12. "Religious Liberties Amendment: Talking Points."

Further Reading

Gay, Kathlyn. *Church and State: Government and Religion in the United States.* Brookfield, Conn.: Millbrook Press, 1991.

Pfeffer, Leo. *Church, State, and Freedom,* rev. ed. Boston: Beacon Press, 1967.

Public Agenda/Kettering Foundation, for National Issues Forums Institute. *Contested Values: Tug-of-War in the School Yard.* Dubuque, Iowa: Kendall/Hunt Publishing Co., 1994.

"Religion in the Public Schools: A Joint Statement of Current Law," a pamphlet published in April 1995 by a coalition of several dozen religious and civil liberties organizations. Copies of the pamphlet can be obtained by writing to: "Religion in the Public Schools" 15 East 84th Street, Suite 501 New York, NY 10028.

Index